Discovering Dinosaurs

Apatosaurus

Aaron Carr

LET'S READ

AV2 BY WEIGL™

ADDED VALUE • AUDIO VISUAL

www.av2books.com

Published by AV² by Weigl
350 5th Avenue, 59th Floor
New York, NY 10118

Website: www.av2books.com   www.weigl.com

Library of Congress Control Number: 2013937447
ISBN 978-1-62127-238-0 (hardcover)
ISBN 978-1-62127-244-1 (softcover)

Printed in the United States of America in North Mankato, Minnesota
1 2 3 4 5 6 7 8 9 0   17 16 15 14 13

052013
WEP040413

Project Coordinator: Aaron Carr
Art Director: Terry Paulhus

All illustrations by Jon Hughes, pixel-shack.com; Getty Images: 19 inset, Dreamstime: 20.

AV² provides enriched content that supplements and complements this book. Weigl's AV² books strive to create inspired learning and engage young minds in a total learning experience.

Your AV² Media Enhanced books come alive with...

Key Words
Study vocabulary, and complete a matching word activity.

Quizzes
Test your knowledge.

Slide Show
View images and captions, and prepare a presentation.

... and much, much more!

Audio
Listen to sections of the book read aloud.

Video
Watch informative video clips.

Embedded Weblinks
Gain additional information for research.

Try This!
Complete activities and hands-on experiments.

AV² by Weigl brings you media enhanced books that support active learning.

BOOK CODE

N333790

Go to www.av2books.com, and enter this book's unique code.

LET'S READ · AV² BY WEIGL™ · ADDED VALUE • AUDIO VISUAL

Apatosaurus

In this book, you will learn

- what its name means
- what it looked like
- where it lived
- what it ate
- and much more!

Meet the Apatosaurus.
Its name means
"deceptive lizard."

Apatosaurus was one of the largest animals ever to live on land.

It weighed more than 70,000 pounds.

7

Apatosaurus had a very long neck. It used its very long neck to reach food.

Apatosaurus was a plant eater. It spent almost all of its time looking for food and eating.

Apatosaurus
did not chew its food.
It used its mouth and teeth
to strip leaves from tree branches.

Apatosaurus
walked very slowly
on its four strong legs.

It may have also
used its tail like an extra leg.

Apatosaurus lived in the middle part of North America.

16

It stayed far away from swamps and other watery places.

Apatosaurus died out more than 137 million years ago.

People know about the Apatosaurus because of fossils.

20

People can go to museums to learn more about the Apatosaurus.

The Age of the Dinosaurs

21

Apatosaurus Facts

These pages provide detailed information that expands on the interesting facts found in the book. They are intended to be used by adults as a learning support to help young readers round out their knowledge of each amazing dinosaur or pterosaur featured in the *Discovering Dinosaurs* series.

Pages 4–5

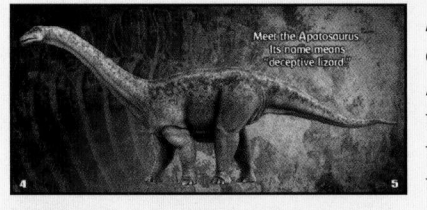

Apatosaurus means "deceptive lizard." Apatosaurus is a massive dinosaur known for its long neck, huge body, and tail. Scientists used to think the Apatosaurus and Brontosaurus were two different dinosaurs. They later learned that Brontosaurus was just a fully-grown Apatosaurus. Since Apatosaurus was the first name given to the species, it is considered the proper name. However, the name Brontosaurus is still sometimes used.

Pages 6–7

Apatosaurus was one of the largest animals ever to live on land. The Apatosaurus weighed as much as 80,000 pounds (36,000 kilograms). Measured from head to tail, the Apatosaurus was up to 70 feet (21 meters) long. Apatosaurus stood 15 feet (4.6 m) tall at the hip. The Apatosaurus was so large, scientists once thought it lived in water to support its weight.

Pages 8–9

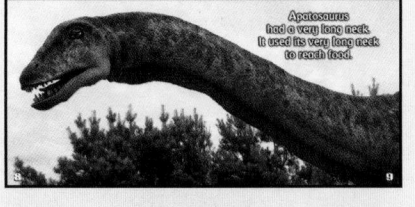

Apatosaurus had a very long neck. Its neck was more than 17 feet (5 m) long. The Apatosaurus used its long neck to graze. Some scientists believe Apatosaurus could raise its head to eat leaves off high tree branches. Others say the extreme length of the neck would have prevented Apatosaurus from raising it more than 17 feet (5 m). Instead, the long neck would have allowed Apatosaurus to reach food in areas its huge body could not go, such as dense forests.

Pages 10–11

Apatosaurus was a herbivore, or plant-eater. The Apatosaurus was one of the largest herbivores ever to live. In order to support its massive size, Apatosaurus would have spent nearly all of its time either searching for food or eating. Tree leaves, conifer seeds, and ferns were some of the plants Apatosaurus ate. Conifers were the dominant plants during the time period in which Apatosaurus lived, so they likely made up most of Apatosaurus's diet.

Apatosaurus did not chew its food. The Apatosaurus used its peg-like teeth to strip leaves and conifer needles from tree branches. It did not use its teeth for chewing. Instead, the Apatosaurus swallowed its food whole. It also swallowed rocks, which stayed in the stomach and helped break down food. Some scientists think Apatosaurus may have had strong lips, like a moose, that would have helped it grasp its food.

Apatosaurus walked very slowly. The Apatosaurus had four huge legs shaped like thick columns. The front legs were slightly shorter than the hind legs. From studying preserved Apatosaurus tracks, scientists know that the dinosaur could only walk very slowly. However, Apatosaurus hatchlings could run quickly on their two hind legs. Some scientists also think Apatosaurus used its tail like a leg. This would have allowed Apatosaurus to stand up on its hind legs, using its tail for added support and balance.

Apatosaurus lived in the middle part of North America.
The Apatosaurus lived in both North America and Europe. In North America, Apatosaurus was found in the middle part of the continent, in the present-day states of Colorado, Utah, Wyoming, and Oklahoma. The massive size of the Apatosaurus meant that it had to live far away from swamps and large bodies of water. This is because it would have sank into the soft ground in these areas.

Apatosaurus died more than 137 million years ago during the Late Jurassic Period. People learned about the Apatosaurus from studying its fossils. Fossils are formed when an animal dies and is quickly covered in sand, mud, or water. This keeps the hard parts of the body, such as bones, teeth and claws, from decomposing. The body is pressed between layers of mud and sand. Over millions of years, the layers turn into stone, and the dinosaur's bones and teeth turn into stone as well. This preserves the size and shape of the dinosaur.

People can go to museums to see fossils and learn more about the Apatosaurus. People from all around the world visit museums each year to see Apatosaurus fossils in person. Not many Apatosaurus fossils have been found, and most of those are not complete. The Carnegie Museum of Natural History in Pittsburgh, Pennsylvania, has a nearly complete Apatosaurus skeleton with a skull. It was discovered in 1909.

KEY WORDS

Research has shown that as much as 65 percent of all written material published in English is made up of 300 words. These 300 words cannot be taught using pictures or learned by sounding them out. They must be recognized by sight. This book contains 54 common sight words to help young readers improve their reading fluency and comprehension. This book also teaches young readers several important content words, such as proper nouns. These words are paired with pictures to aid in learning and improve understanding.

Page	Sight Words First Appearance
5	its, means, name, the
6	animals, land, live, of, on, one, to, was
7	it, more, than
9	a, food, had, long, used, very
10	all, almost, and, for, plant, time
12	and, did, from, not, tree
14	four, walked
15	also, an, have, like, may
16	in, part
17	away, far, places, other
18	out, years
19	about, because, know, people
20	can, go, learn

Page	Content Words First Appearance
5	Apatosaurus (pronounced: ah-PAT-uh-SAWR-us), lizard
7	pounds
9	neck
10	eater
12	branches, leaves, mouth, teeth
14	legs
15	tail
16	North America
17	swamps
19	fossils
20	museums